FAMA

Monologue of a Zillenial

First edition

This book was professionally typeset on Reedsy.
Find out more at reedsy.com

Contents

Prologue

This isn't a self-help guide. There are no five-step plans to financial freedom, no bullet-point lists for achieving ultimate zen in a world that feels perpetually on fire. This is just a conversation. A monologue, if you will, but one echoing in a crowded, noisy room where, if you listen closely enough, you might hear a thousand other voices whispering the exact same bewildered questions.

If you're holding this, or reading it on a screen, chances are you know the feeling. The chronological whiplash. The messy attic of a brain where dial-up tones live alongside 5G. The bewildering dance between a pre-digital childhood and a hyper-connected, hyper-anxious adulthood. You're likely hovering somewhere between your mid-twenties and early thirties, a Zillennial, a hybrid, a bridge generation that remembers both Blockbuster and TikTok, believing you are alone in this weird, accelerated timeline.

But here's the secret, whispered between the lines of this little book, between the chapters of a life that often feels like a glitching server: **you are not alone.** Not in the frantic job hunt, not in the housing market despair, not in the quiet exhaustion of constant self-branding, and certainly not in the creeping suspicion that "adulthood" is just a performance none of us have truly mastered. The same existential dread that keeps you up at 3 AM is likely keeping someone else up, two towns over, three continents away, or even in the apartment directly above yours.

This isn't a definitive answer to the chaos; it's an acknowledgement of it. A nod of understanding from one tired, hopeful, slightly sarcastic soul to another. Consider this a shared moment of recognition, a collective sigh. We've all been handed a map to a world that no longer exists, and this monologue is about the glorious, frustrating, often hilarious journey of trying to navigate without one. It's about the quiet rebellion, the search for authentic connection in a hyper-real world, and the unscripted adventure of simply trying to exist when everything tells you to hustle.

So, settle in. Take a deep breath. You don't need to have it all figured out. In fact, perhaps the most powerful thing we can do is admit that we don't. Because in that shared vulnerability, in that collective, bewildered question mark, we might just find the quiet, steady hum of connection we've all been searching for. This isn't just my story; it's *our* story. And it's just beginning.

1

The Hybrid Generation

I'm pretty sure I exist in a state of chronological whiplash. My brain is a messy attic filled with a perfectly balanced mix of dial-up tones and the ungodly speed of 5G. I remember when the biggest decision of my life was whether to use a cheat code on Age of Empires or just grind it out. The sound of a Windows 95 startup still feels more comforting than a lullaby. We were the last generation to get kicked out of the house with a "be back before the streetlights come on" and the first to get sucked into the black mirror of the internet. We still know how to build a fort out of sticks, but we're also fluent in meme culture and the dark arts of a well-timed GIF.

The music. Oh, the music. It was the soundtrack to our split-screen existence. One moment we were listening to Blink-182 while skateboarding (or, let's be honest, just sitting on the curb), the next we were getting hyped to Usher on our first MP3 player with a whopping 256MB of storage. It was a chaotic symphony of pop-punk angst and bubblegum pop confidence, and it made perfect sense at the time.

But now? Now everything feels like it's being played on fast-forward. The year 2020 hit, and it was like someone flipped the "afterburner" switch on the universe. The decades before felt like a slow, meandering stroll through a park, and now the years are just flashing by like highway signs in a blur. The psychological disconnect is wild. I'm almost 30, but I still instinctively think I have to ask my mom for permission to get something from the store. My inner voice is a panicked teen, while my external life is demanding things like "retirement planning" and "stable housing." What? I still haven't figured out how to fold a fitted sheet.

The economic situation is a punchline, except nobody's laughing. We were sold a promise of a future where hard work paid off, but the reality feels more like a game of musical chairs where someone keeps taking away the chairs. The housing market is a fantasy novel. The jobs we were told would save us are now being threatened by AI that is learning to do our jobs better than we ever could. My parents bought a house for a third of my annual salary, and now I'm looking at a down payment that costs more than my entire life savings. It's a chaotic, nonsensical spiral of inflation, climate anxiety, and the creeping feeling that we're the first generation to be worse off than our parents.

I'm not saying we're suffering more than anyone else, but it's a unique brand of chaos. We've had a front-row seat to the rapid acceleration of technology, society, and global issues, all while trying to navigate the mundane-yet-impossible tasks of adulthood. What will happen to my career? Have I had all the fun I'm supposed to have? What is actually going on?

The only answer I've found so far is that maybe it's okay for things to not make sense. Maybe the shared, chaotic experience of growing up with one foot in the pre-digital world and one in the hyper-connected now is the only thing we have. Maybe the true monologue of a zillennial is just a single, bewildered question mark, followed by a wry, self-deprecating laugh.

2

The Sound of Subscription

Remember when music was a physical object? A CD with a jewel case so delicate it felt like it could shatter if you looked at it funny. The satisfying *thunk* of a cassette deck. The ritual of flipping through a booklet filled with blurry band photos and lyrics you couldn't quite decipher. My first jobs were not about career-building; they were about funding a library of sound. It was an investment. I still remember the first CD I ever bought with my own money—Linkin Park's *Hybrid Theory*. The title feels a little too on the nose now. I didn't just listen to the music; I owned it. It was a tangible asset, a precious object you had to handle with reverence. The music wasn't just data; it was a physical part of our lives, organized into shrines of leaning towers in our bedrooms.

Then came the internet, and with it, the great aural anarchy. We became digital pirates, not out of malice, but because the alternative was waiting for a CD to come out on a Tuesday and then scrounging up enough pocket money to buy it. We lived in the Wild West of Limewire and Kazaa. The thrill of a song download was a glorious gamble. Was it the full song?

Was it a corrupted file that sounded like a robot choking on gravel? Or was it a five-minute recording of a dial-up modem screaming into the void? The emotional rollercoaster was a rite of passage. In the end, we went from owning our music to a monthly subscription that offers everything and feels like nothing.

This shift from **ownership** to **access** wasn't just about music. It's the defining psychological shift of our generation. My parents bought a house in their twenties. A house. Something with a roof, a yard, and a mortgage that actually got smaller over time. My version of that is a monthly rent payment that feels less like I'm building equity and more like I'm just leasing my right to exist in a specific geographic location. Retirement? Please. That's a concept for our Boomer parents. Our retirement plan is a meme, a bitter joke passed around on social media. We were sold a dream—go to college, get a degree, find a job, buy a house, retire. We followed the instructions to the letter, got the degrees, and then found out the game had been patched. The rules had changed, and the entire economy was a broken, glitching server. We're over-educated, under-employed, and living in a world that feels like an ever-increasing list of monthly subscriptions.

We're a generation that got dressed up for the prom just to find out the school was on fire. We've got the education, the work ethic, and the skills, but we're playing a rigged game. The fun, carefree music of our youth feels like a cruel, ironic soundtrack to a very real, very tangible economic pressure cooker. It's a bitter joke, isn't it? The same songs that remind us of simpler times are now playing on a streaming service we can barely afford, while we're stuck in a loop of panic about a future we can't seem to grab a hold of.

The feeling of being a teenager hasn't really gone away. I'm almost thirty, and my internal monologue is still a chaotic mix of "Did I turn off the stove?" and "I wonder if my crush saw my Instagram story." We're the first generation to hit our thirties and still feel like we're in the extended pilot episode of our lives. Everyone else seems to be on Season 3, Episode 12, with a clear plot and character development, but we're just... here. The 'career ladder' is no longer a ladder; it's a greased pole with no handholds and a hundred other people trying to climb it at the same time. We've replaced a stable job with a series of "gigs" and "side hustles," which is a fancy way of saying we're all freelance everything, desperately trying to assemble a coherent life from a pile of digital breadcrumbs. And while we're doing this, our boomer parents are asking why we just don't "pick a path." A path? The whole forest is on fire! We're just trying to not get burned.

This gig economy, this "freelance" existence, is a twisted evolution of the choose-your-own-adventure book. Except now, every page-turn feels less like a choice and more like a desperate attempt to stay afloat. One minute, you're a "social media consultant," the next you're a "brand evangelist," which, in my experience, is just a polite way of saying "person who gets paid ten dollars to post about coffee on their personal account." Our resumes look less like a career progression and more like a schizophrenic list of hobbies we convinced someone to pay us for. It's a constant performance, a never-ending cycle of self-branding and networking. You're not just an employee; you're an entrepreneur, a creator, a personal brand. It's exhausting. We're all wearing a dozen different hats, and none of them fit properly. We're perpetually on the brink of burnout, chugging lukewarm coffee and staring at spreadsheets with a thousand tabs open. Our lives are a browser with too many windows, all running in the background and slowing down the whole system.

3

The Great Acceleration

The year 2020. The great global pause. We all thought it would be a blip, a temporary setback before a triumphant return to normalcy. Instead, it was like someone hit a global reset button and then immediately cranked the speed up to 11. Time, which was once a linear, predictable river, became a frantic, churning whirlpool. March 2020 felt like five years long, and then the next five years disappeared in the blink of an eye. Was that last year? Or five years ago? I can't even remember. The timelines have blurred, and my memory feels less like a filing cabinet and more like a junk drawer overflowing with random receipts and old batteries.

It's a peculiar kind of psychological warfare. We spent months in a state of suspended animation, and then when the world opened up again, it was a blur of Zoom calls and "pivots" and "new normals." The sense of existential dread that had been simmering for years finally boiled over. The economy felt like a house of cards, constantly on the verge of collapse. Our careers, once a slow and steady climb, became a frantic game of musical chairs. Every job felt temporary, every layoff a matter of "when," not "if." We're not just worried about our next paycheck; we're worried about the entire system. We've inherited a world that feels fragile, a society with more questions than answers.

There's a constant, low-grade hum of anxiety that we all carry. It's the unspoken understanding that the ground beneath our feet is a little shakier than we were told. We look at our parents' generation, who bought a house and had a family on a single salary, and we wonder if we've somehow failed, even though the game we're playing is entirely different. We've had all the fun, haven't we? The concerts, the trips, the carefree nights. Now, as we approach our thirties, the party feels like it's over, and we're left to clean up the mess. And the worst part? We don't even know where the trash cans are.

And then there's the technology, a relentless tide that just keeps rising. My phone is a little black mirror of societal collapse, a portal to a world on fire, and I can't stop staring at it. I've gone from checking the news once a day to doomscrolling for hours, absorbing a cascade of information that makes me feel simultaneously more informed and utterly helpless. The digital world that was our escape is now the primary source of our anxiety. It's like we've been given all the answers, but none of them make any sense. We've replaced the simple question of "what will I do tomorrow?" with the impossible question of "what's going on with the entire planet?" and the cognitive dissonance is enough to short-circuit a supercomputer. We are the ultimate beta testers, running a buggy and unstable version of society and just hoping it doesn't crash on us completely.

And then there's the social media performance. We're not just living our lives; we're curating them. Every meal, every vacation, every minor accomplishment is a potential piece of content to be uploaded and optimized for likes. We grew up with friends whose flaws you knew by heart because you saw them every day. Now, our friendships are a series of perfectly edited highlight reels, a constant stream of "I'm having a better time than you" from people we've never actually had a conversation with. It's all part of the same weird, chaotic experiment. We're living our lives in front of an audience of strangers and a ghost of our past, trying to figure out what's real and what's just a glitch in the simulation.

4

The Hustle

The career ladder is a myth. It's a drawing on a whiteboard in a corporate office that hasn't been used since 2008. We were told to climb it, but we got to the office and found it had been replaced by a series of high-stakes, ill-defined obstacle courses. Now, our resumes look less like a career progression and more like a schizophrenic list of hobbies we convinced someone to pay us for. "Social Media Ninja." "Growth Hacker." "Brand Evangelist." These aren't jobs; they're personality archetypes. And we're all supposed to be a dozen of them at once. It's exhausting, this performance. We're perpetually on the brink of burnout, chugging lukewarm coffee and staring at spreadsheets with a thousand tabs open, each one a different "gig" or "side hustle."

This "freelance" existence is a twisted evolution of the choose-your-own-adventure book. Except now, every page-turn feels less like a choice and more like a desperate attempt to stay afloat. One minute, you're a "digital nomad," the next you're just a person with a laptop at Starbucks who hasn't made rent in three months. The idea of a stable, 9-to-5 job feels as quaint as a horse-drawn carriage. The constant pressure to be "on," to be networking, to be building your "personal brand," is a full-time job in itself. You're not just an employee; you're an entrepreneur, a creator, a publicist, and a brand manager for the most high-maintenance brand you know: yourself.

We're all wearing a dozen different hats, and none of them fit properly. We're told to find our passion and turn it into a paycheck, but sometimes, a hobby is just a hobby. And the moment it becomes a "hustle," it loses all the joy. It's a comedy of errors, a perpetual game of catch-up. We watch older generations retire and wonder if that's even a possibility for us. It's hard to save for a future when the present is on fire. Our lives are a browser with too many windows, all running in the background and slowing down the whole system. And for some reason, the system is still buffering.

And then there's the work-from-home irony. We finally got the "flexibility" we've been asking for, but it feels less like a perk and more like a cage. My living room is now a conference room, and my bedroom is a second office. There's no separation anymore. The line between work and life didn't just blur; it evaporated. You're always on call, always one Slack message away from a panic attack. The freedom to work in your pajamas is just a new way to be a prisoner of your inbox, and the coffee break is now a frantic dash to the kitchen to microwave your cold coffee while trying to look attentive on a video call. It's a different kind of performance, a silent audition where you're trying to look productive without anyone actually seeing you.

The societal pressures feel more intense than ever. Social media has become a highlight reel of everyone else's "best life." Everyone is a "founder" or a "consultant" or a "creator," and their perfectly curated feeds tell a story of non-stop success.

We're constantly comparing our messy, chaotic realities to their polished, edited fictions. It's a race we didn't sign up for, a constant reminder that we're not doing enough, not earning enough, and not living up to our "potential." We've been told our whole lives that we can be anything, but that pressure has turned into a paralyzing fear of not being everything.

5

The Digital Audience

Not everyone is a creator, but we're all audiences. We're the ones scrolling, double-tapping, and consuming the endless stream of content, and that's a different kind of performance. We're watching everyone else's highlight reel—the perfect vacation, the sparkling clean home, the effortlessly successful career—and it's hard not to feel like our own lives are a little less than. It's a peculiar kind of psychological fatigue. We're not just seeing the world; we're seeing a hyper-curated, perfectly edited version of it, and we're comparing our raw, unedited reality to it every single day.

The algorithm doesn't just demand content; it demands our attention. It's a master manipulator, learning our desires and fears and feeding us a perfectly curated world that reinforces what we already believe. It's a feedback loop of our own making, and the more we consume, the more we become a part of the machine. The digital world that was once our playground has become a gilded cage, and we're the ones who have been staring at the bars all along.

The distinction between the public and private self has

vanished. Our lives are an open browser, and every tab is a different performance. We're living in a world of algorithms, and the algorithms aren't just selling us products; they're telling us who we should be. They've learned our habits, our desires, our fears, and they're feeding us a perfectly curated version of the world that only reinforces our existing beliefs. It's a feedback loop of our own making, and the more we engage, the more we become a part of the machine. The digital world that was once our playground has become a gilded cage, and we're the ones who have been putting on the show all along.

6

The Quiet Rebellion

After all this, you'd think we'd be completely broken. Overwhelmed by the chaos, paralyzed by the anxiety, and lost in the digital noise. But something else is happening. It's a quiet rebellion, a slow but steady pushback against the madness. It's the moment when you close the laptop, turn off the phone, and just... exist. We've been living in a world of constant connection, and now we're rediscovering the beauty of being disconnected.

The rebellion isn't a grand protest or a viral hashtag. It's a quiet, personal decision. It's about reading a physical book with paper pages and no pop-up ads. It's about cooking a meal for the sheer pleasure of it, not for the perfect Instagram photo. It's about sitting in a room with a friend and having a conversation that isn't interrupted by a push notification. We're not just nostalgic for the past; we're actively trying to bring parts of it back. We're rediscovering the joy of slowness, the comfort of tangibility, and the power of being present.

It's the small, sensory details that bring us back to ourselves. The weight of a coffee cup in your hands. The smell of rain on pavement. The feeling of grass between your toes. These aren't experiences you can "like" or "share," and they're all the more powerful for it. They remind us that our world isn't a flat, glowing screen, but a vibrant, three-dimensional space filled with textures, scents, and sounds. They are our personal, non-optimized anchors in a sea of data.

The greatest casualty of the digital age isn't just our attention spans; it's our sense of community. We have thousands of followers, but how many people can we call when the metaphorical car breaks down? The quiet rebellion is about rebuilding those connections, one meaningful conversation at a time. It's about showing up, not just in an online forum, but on a front porch with a six-pack. It's about trading likes for laughs and comments for companionship.

This rebellion, ultimately, is about reclaiming our own humanity. It's about choosing to be a person, not a profile. We've been told our whole lives that we can be anything, and maybe the most powerful thing we can be is just ourselves, navigating the chaos with a little humor and a whole lot of heart. We're the bridge between two worlds, and maybe, just maybe, we're the ones who can finally fix the buffering.

7

Hyper-reality

We're all living in a constant feedback loop of images and narratives, and it's getting harder to tell the original from the copy. The internet didn't just add a layer to our reality; it created a new, hyper-real one. This is the world of filters that make a sunrise look more beautiful than it was in person, of news events that feel more like a movie plot than a tangible occurrence, and of lives that are more real online than off. It's a world where our experiences are often secondary to their documentation, and we don't truly feel like we've lived a moment until we've posted it. The real question is: are we living for the moment, or are we just living for the 'gram?

The line between simulation and reality has blurred to the point of being non-existent. We're watching our lives play out on a screen, and the world itself feels like a high-definition rendering of something that used to be messy and real. We consume news, art, and human connection through a series of perfectly curated feeds, and everything feels both more vivid and more distant. Our anxiety isn't just about economic precarity; it's about the unsettling feeling that we're all just actors in a collective performance, and none of us can remember our lines. The world we were born into is gone, replaced by a simulation that's so good it's terrifyingly real.

We've become experts at being in character, at presenting a version of ourselves that is more palatable, more successful, and more composed than our actual, messy selves. We've internalized the idea that our lives are a narrative, and every decision is a plot point. This constant self-editing, this endless performance, creates a deep and quiet disconnect—the feeling that the person in the mirror is a stranger who lives for the approval of an unseen audience. It's a type of psychic jet lag, where our physical and digital selves are never quite in the same time zone.

This performative life extends to our emotions. We no longer just feel something; we format it for public consumption. Grief isn't just a personal journey; it's a series of somber posts and carefully selected photos. Joy isn't a spontaneous outburst; it's a reel set to a trending audio track, meticulously edited to look effortless. This commodification of feeling creates a bizarre distance from our own inner lives, making even our most profound experiences feel like just another piece of content. We are both the subject and the director of our own personal reality show, and the constant need to "perform" our humanity is a tiring, hollow task.

This is all made more complex by the arrival of generative AI. The simulation is now creating its own content. The line between a human-curated highlight reel and an AI-generated fiction is starting to blur. A viral image might be a photograph or a text prompt. A moving piece of writing might be from a person or a sophisticated algorithm. This layer of ambiguity is the final piece of the hypereality puzzle. It's no longer just about us performing for an audience; it's about us trying to find the human heart in a world that is increasingly populated by beautifully rendered fakes.

And perhaps that's why we're so tired. The exhaustion isn't just from the pace of life or the constant stream of bad news; it's from the effort of living a double life. We're navigating both a real world and a hyper-real world, and we're expected to be perfectly at home in both. We're the only generation that remembers a time before it was a performance, which means we're also the only ones who can see the seams, the little cracks where the simulation breaks. We're not just consumers of this new reality; we're its unintended critics, pointing out the glitches and searching for the lost source code. We're not just a generation of survivors; we're a generation of critics, constantly deconstructing the performance and looking for the authentic moments hiding beneath the pixels. And maybe, in our quiet rebellion, we're not just trying to escape the chaos—we're trying to find our way back to what's real.

8

The Unseen Weight

We've inherited a world on the brink, and every instinct tells us to fix it. We've got a thousand ideas for a more sustainable future, a more equitable society, a kinder way of living. We're full of plans for protests and policies and innovative new businesses. But there's this unseen weight in the air, a kind of collective paralysis. The issues feel too big, too complex, and too ingrained to tackle. It's a frustration that's both individual and generational—the feeling that we're holding a fire extinguisher in our hands, but the building is already a pile of ashes, and we're not even sure where to point it. We want to be the generation that makes a difference, but we're so busy just surviving that the grand, heroic gestures feel impossible.

But we do it anyway. Not with a bang, but with a thousand small, quiet acts of defiance. We might not be able to fix the global climate crisis, but we can start a community garden. We can't dismantle systemic inequality overnight, but we can have difficult, empathetic conversations with our family. We're finding our way through the rubble, not with a pre-written plan, but with an improvised dance. It's a stubborn, gritty kind of hope, born not from optimism but from the sheer refusal to give up. We're not the ones who will write the history books, but we're the ones who will live the small, messy, beautiful stories that will get us through it all. And maybe, just maybe, those stories are what the world needs the most.

We scroll through headlines like they're tombstones: extinction rates, melting ice sheets, algorithmic oppression, housing unaffordability, the gig economy eating careers like Pac-Man on a sugar rush. And every time we try to *do something*, the system hisses back: *You don't own a home. You have student debt. You're replaceable.* So we retreat—not out of apathy, but out of exhaustion. It's not that we don't care; it's that caring feels like holding your breath underwater while the surface keeps getting farther away. We're not lazy, we're *overqualified for despair*. But then, somewhere between therapy co-pays and grocery inflation, we do the smallest thing: we compost. We vote in local elections. We text a friend who's been quiet. We start a mutual aid fund on a Google Sheet. These aren't revolutions—they're rebellions in slow motion. And somehow, they keep the light on.

There's a quiet revolution happening in the cracks of this broken world, and we're its accidental architects. We don't wear capes or give TED Talks (unless it's for exposure). We're the ones organizing potlucks for climate fundraisers, sharing job leads in group chats, fostering rescue dogs because pets are the only dependents we can afford. We've stopped waiting for permission to be heroes. Instead, we've redefined heroism: it's showing up to a friend's art show even when you're burnt out; it's choosing to plant flowers in a war zone of concrete; it's saying "I don't know" and still trying anyway. We may never save the world as we were promised we could—but we're building something quieter, deeper, more human. Not a utopia. Just *enough*. And in a world that demands everything, sometimes *enough* is the most radical thing of all.

9

The Disconnected Connection

You'd think, with a phone full of contacts and a feed full of "friends," that we'd never be lonely. But the loneliness now feels deeper, a silent hum underneath the constant noise. We're all in our separate little digital bubbles, scrolling through a stream of perfectly curated lives, and it's easy to feel like you're the only one who's not winning. We're sharing highlights, not heartaches. We're communicating in fragmented snippets, not real conversations. It's like we're all shouting into a crowded room, but no one is actually listening. The irony is staggering: we have more ways to connect than ever before, and we feel more isolated.

The real tragedy is that we're all too busy to actually connect. The pace of life has gone from a sprint to a blur, and there's no finish line in sight. We're all hustling, grinding, and chasing the next promotion, the next paycheck, the next social media milestone. Our friendships get relegated to a text message here, a quick DM there. We see our closest friends as tiny thumbnails in an app, not as real people who need a real conversation. In the rush to do everything, to be everything, we've forgotten how to simply be present with the people who matter most. The fast-paced life has stolen our time, our energy, and our ability to build something meaningful.The existential dread is palpable, the feeling that you're supposed to be somewhere, doing something, but you have no idea what that is

And at 27, it all feels a bit ridiculous, doesn't it? You're supposed to have it all figured out, but you're still just trying to find your footing.Here's the dirty little secret no one talks about: the older generations don't actually have it together. That calm, confident aura your parents project? That uncle who says, "Back in my day, we just worked hard and things worked out"? Yeah, they're faking it too. Turns out, adulthood isn't a switch you flip at 30—it's a series of increasingly complex compromises, quiet regrets, and pretending you know how to unclog a garbage disposal. We've mythologized previous generations as wise, stable, and self-assured, but the truth is, they were just as confused as we are—only with less therapy and more smoking. They didn't have answers; they just moved forward anyway, often silently, often lonely, often broke. The difference? They didn't have Instagram to remind them, every five minutes, that someone else apparently does.

So when we feel like we're failing because we're not homeowners, CEOs, or emotionally enlightened beings by 28, let's remember: no one ever was. The myth of "having it all figured out" is just that—a myth. The older folks aren't laughing at us; they're quietly Googling "how to talk to your adult child about credit scores" and wondering if they raised us right. The difference is, we're doing it out loud. We're naming the anxiety. We're texting "I'm not okay" instead of bottling it up for 30 years. We're asking for help. And that? That's not weakness. That's evolution. Maybe our version of connection isn't grand dinners or lifelong neighbors. Maybe it's a 2 a.m. voice note, a meme that says exactly what words can't, or showing up to a friend's apartment with soup and silence. We may be disconnected by design, but we're redefining what it means to be close. And sometimes, that's enough—to be seen, to be heard, to say, "Yeah, I'm lost too. Want to get coffee and be lost together?"

Maybe the purpose isn't a single destination, but the messy, beautiful journey of getting through it all. We're the generation that's navigating the impossible, and in the quiet moments between the digital noise, we're finding that the most important connection we can make is with ourselves.

10

The Unscripted Adventure

We've been taught our whole lives that there's a script. A predefined set of instructions that tells us how to live, what to become, and when to get there. Let's be real: the script was never real. It was a PowerPoint presentation handed down by boomers who peaked in the '90s and still think "digital nomad" means someone who uses a laptop at Starbucks. That script said: Graduate → Get a job → Buy a house → Marry → Have 2.5 kids → Retire at 65. But the world changed. The economy imploded. Jobs became gigs. Houses became unattainable fantasy castles. And suddenly, we're all wandering around like NPCs in a game that forgot to give us a quest log. But here's the twist—maybe not having a script is the upgrade. Maybe the freedom to make our own path, even if it's paved with uncertainty and side hustles, is the gift hidden in the chaos. We're not failing the script—we're rewriting it, one awkward pivot at a time. Who knew being lost could feel so liberating?

And in the quiet moments—when the phone is down, the Wi-Fi is off, and the world stops demanding—we start to notice something strange: we're actually kind of okay. Not "I've achieved enlightenment" okay, but "I made it through another Tuesday" okay. And that counts. We're learning to measure success not in promotions or likes, but in small rebellions: saying no without guilt, taking a nap without shame, crying at a dog food commercial and not pretending we weren't. We're discovering that meaning isn't found in some grand finale, but in the in-between—laughing with a friend over burnt ramen, texting your sister a meme that says "I love you but I can't," or just standing in the kitchen, staring out the window, feeling the sun on your face and thinking, "I'm here. I'm alive. And somehow, that's enough." The adventure isn't out there. It's in this—imperfect, unplanned, and utterly ours.

We're supposed to find the answers—the perfect career, the ideal partner, the stable future. But what if the whole point is that there are no answers? What if the map has been torn up, the script is just a series of scribbles, and we're all just improvising? It's a terrifying thought, but it's also an exhilarating one. This isn't a test with a pass or fail grade; it's an experience. It's messy and chaotic and confusing, and it might be a little bit shitty sometimes, but it's ours.

Maybe the point isn't to have it all figured out, but to feel it all. To sit in the discomfort of not knowing. To embrace the ridiculousness of it all. To find the humor in the chaos and the meaning in the struggle. This is our adventure, and the thrill of it isn't in the destination but in the unpredictable turns along the way. We can't control the future, but we can choose how we show up for the present. We can choose to be fully here, even when "here" feels like a strange and confusing place.

And those voices in our head, the ones telling us we're not enough, that we're falling behind? Maybe they won't ever go away completely, but maybe, just maybe, they won't be so loud and confused anymore. Maybe they'll become a gentle murmur instead of a frantic shout. Maybe we'll learn to listen to them with a little more compassion and a little less fear. Maybe we'll learn that the most important journey we can ever take isn't a flight to a new city or a climb up a corporate ladder, but the journey back to ourselves. And for a generation that's been told we're supposed to have all the answers, learning to live in the question might be the most valuable thing of all.

www.ingramcontent.com/pod-product-compliance
Lightning Source LLC
LaVergne TN
LVHW090336210926
848480LV00004B/1436
9798232493646